# THE
# EXPLORER
## THROUGH HISTORY

Julia Waterlow

with illustrations by Tony Smith

Thomson Learning
New York

# JOURNEY THROUGH HISTORY
## The Builder Through History
## The Explorer Through History
## The Farmer Through History
## The Inventor Through History
## The Sailor Through History
## The Soldier Through History

First published in the
United States in 1994 by
Thomson Learning
115 Fifth Avenue
New York, NY 10003

First published in 1994 by
Wayland (Publishers) Limited

UK version copyright © 1994
Wayland (Publishers) Limited

U.S. version copyright © 1994
Thomson Learning

Library of Congress Cataloging-in-
Publication Data
Waterlow, Julia.
   The explorer through history / Julia
Waterlow ; with illustrations by Tony
Smith.
      p.    cm.—(Journey through history)
   Includes bibliographical references
and index.
   Summary: Examines the history of
human exploration, from the ancient
Egyptians to today's astronauts.
   ISBN 1-56847-101-7
   1. Discoveries in geography—History—
Juvenile Literature. 2. Explorers—
Juvenile literature. [1. Discoveries in
geography—History. 2. Explorers.] I.
Smith, Tony, ill. II. Title. III. Series.
G175.W38        1994
910'.92—dc20              93-5656

Printed in Italy

**Text acknowledgments**
The publishers have attempted to
contact all copyright holders of the
quotations in this book, and
apologize if there have been any
oversights. The publishers
gratefully acknowledge permission
from the following to reproduce
copyright material: BBC Books, for
extracts reproduced from *Explorers*,
by Desmond Wilcox, 1975, with the
permission of BBC Enterprises Ltd.;
Ian Allen, for extracts from *Apollo
11 Moon Landing*, by David J.
Shayler, 1989; McGraw-Hill Inc.
New York, for extracts from *The
Discoverers: An Encyclopedia of
Explorers and Exploration*, by
Helen Delpar, 1980; Macdonald, for
an extract from *For All Mankind*, by
Harry Hurt III, 1989; Macmillan, for
extracts from *Life of Mary Kingsley*,
by Stephen Gwynn, 1932; Extracts
from *The Travels of Captain Cook*,
© Ronald Syme, 1972 reproduced
by permission of Michael Joseph
Ltd.; Mitchell Beazley, for an extract
from *World Atlas of Exploration*, by
Eric Newby, 1975; Routledge and
Kegan Paul, for extracts from *Ibn
Battuta: Travels in Asia and Africa*,
1983; Penguin Books, for extracts
from *Marco Polo: The Travels*,
translated by R. Latham, 1975, ©
Ronald Latham, 1958.

**Picture acknowledgments**
The publishers and author wish to
thank Archiv Für Kunst und
Geschichte, Berlin 5 (British
Library, London), 16 and 17
(Bibliothèque Nationale, Paris), 21,
24, 25, 37; Bridgeman Art Library
*cover* (top), 18; Mary Evans Picture
Library 14, 28; Sir Ranulph Fiennes
4; Michael Holford 6, 12, 22; Image
Select 38, 40; Peter Newark's
Historical Pictures 30, 32, 33, 36;
Ann Ronan at Image Select 29;
Topham Picture Library *cover*
(bottom), 41 (top), 42, 44, 45; Julia
Waterlow 34; Wayland Picture
Library 26; Werner Forman Archive
8 (Iraq Museum, Baghdad), 10
(Viking Ship Museum, Oslo).

# Contents

# Into the unknown

Explorers have played an important part in forming the world we know. The routes they pioneered have brought people from every corner of the planet in touch with one another. Civilizations have met with happy and tragic results, but there is no doubting the bravery of those who crossed unknown lands and seas and made the first contact.

It is difficult to imagine how difficult and dangerous journeys were even a couple of hundred years ago. Modern equipment, food, and

**Above** Sir Ranulph Fiennes, an English explorer, led an expedition across the Antarctic in 1993.

medicines now keep travelers relatively comfortable, fit, healthy, and safe – even in bad conditions. Radio and satellite communications allow modern explorers to be in touch with outside help, and in an emergency helicopters can often come to the rescue.

Early pathfinders had none of these aids to help them. They had to be physically tough to make land journeys on foot or on horseback across deserts, through forests, and over mountains. There was no certainty of shelter at night or of a next meal.

A sea voyage could be worse. The first ships hugged the coast, their crews afraid to lose sight of land and be swept out to where they thought monsters were lying in wait. When later sailors ventured out into the oceans, their journeys were often uncomfortable and miserable. Vikings who crossed the northern

## Who were the explorers?

Many of the explorers in this book are European. Although in the past other peoples have explored new lands, Europeans have kept better records of their journeys, so more is known about them. When the Portuguese, the great sea explorers of the sixteenth century, first arrived in Ceylon (now Sri Lanka, near India), the local people were amazed at their strange, restless energy and desire to travel.

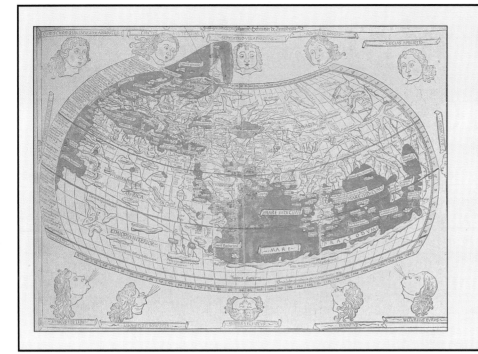

**Ptolemy's map of the world**
This is a fifteenth-century version of one of the first maps of the world. The Greek geographer Claudius Ptolemaeus Ptolemy drew it in the second century A.D., and it was still the standard map used in Europe when Christopher Columbus set sail in 1492. The map does not show any land west of Europe. When people realized that the world was round they thought that China could be reached by sailing across the Atlantic Ocean.

Modern maps look very different and are more detailed because explorers have gone to different lands and then described their journeys.

seas in their open-topped boats must have been extremely wet and cold.

Without today's maps and aids to navigation, explorers could often get lost or be unsure about their location. Although the fifteenth century Italian explorer Christopher Columbus managed to sail back and forth across the Atlantic Ocean, he thought to his dying day that he had landed near China or the Indies. He did not know that the continents we now call the Americas existed. For many sea explorers these hard journeys also meant death from illness: until the time of Captain Cook no one realized that fresh food could help prevent the disease scurvy.

There are many reasons people explore. Throughout history the desire for trade has sparked journeys to unfamiliar places. Some, like the Spanish conquistadores, made long voyages to unknown lands to conquer and plunder riches; others, such as the Vikings who crossed the Atlantic, searched for new homes; and a number of the great Arab travelers were inspired by religion.

Over the last two hundred years or so, as the world has finally been mapped and only the details need to be filled in, there have been new kinds of explorers. Scientists or people who are just extremely curious about the world around them travel for study or enjoyment. Throughout the ages though, explorers have had in common the excitement and challenges of the unknown.

**The compass**
A compass is a vital piece of equipment for exploration because it shows the direction of magnetic north. Although the Chinese had discovered the principles of the compass in the second century B.C., they did not use it as a traveling aid until much later. When Europeans started using it in the thirteenth century A.D., it was just a magnetized needle attached to a piece of wood floating in water.

# The pioneering Phoenicians

In about 450 B.C., it is said, sixty ships carrying thousands of colonists, their belongings, and supplies set out into the unknown from the Phoenician city of Carthage. These Carthaginians sailed from their home on the north coast of Africa (modern Tunisia), out into the Atlantic Ocean, and down the west coast of Africa.

Under the command of a man named Hanno, they set up new trading colonies at several points along the African coast. With this accomplished, Hanno decided to continue exploring.

He sailed inland up a large river (possibly the Senegal River), seeing hippopotamuses and crocodiles and passing high mountains. Farther south, back along the coast, he and his crew heard "the sound of pipes and cymbals, the rumble of drums, and mighty cries" coming out of the dense forest. Scared, the explorers sped past.

Beyond, Hanno describes coming across a burning mountain, which he named the Chariot of the Gods. This volcano may have been Mount Cameroon in modern West Cameroon.

Where they found friendly inhabitants, they traded their cargoes. But neither valuable land nor goods were found, and the Carthaginians returned home. It was another 2,000 years before outsiders went to explore the area again.

**Below** This stone carving, dating from about 700 B.C., shows a ship built and crewed by Phoenicians.

### The Phoenician ship
The Phoenicians were known as the greatest sailors of the ancient Mediterranean world. A Greek historian said, "Once I had an opportunity of looking over a great Phoenician merchantman [a type of ship] …and I thought I had never seen tackle so excellently and accurately arranged." Most ships had covered decks with a single sail, and two banks of oars manned by thirty to fifty oarsmen. They carried huge cargoes and weapons to defend themselves.

**BRITAIN**

**EUROPE**

**ASIA**

**SPAIN**
Gades

Carthage

**PHOENICIA**

**EGYPT**

**AFRICA**

Senegal
River

Mount Cameroon

→ Himilco's route
→ Phoenician trade routes
→ Hanno's route

The Phoenician explorer Hanno at the prow (front) of his ship. He set out on an expedition in 450 B.C. to explore the west coast of Africa, lands completely unknown to people of the Mediterranean Sea.

**Land of flames**
As Hanno sailed along the coast of Africa, he described "a burning yet sweet-smelling region where streams of fire ran out into the sea. We could not go ashore because of the heat…
On the four nights following we saw land covered in flames. In the center of the land was a high pyre, larger than the others, which seemed to reach to the stars." It may well have been a volcano, possibly Mount Cameroon, that the Carthaginian explorers saw erupting.

## The pioneering Phoenicians

Phoenicia was a thin strip of land along the east coast of the Mediterranean Sea (approximately the area of present-day Lebanon). The Phoenicians were the greatest merchants of their time, with trading routes crossing both land and water. They became masters of the Mediterranean, and sailed and explored the area from one end to the other. Their skill as sailors is mentioned in the Old Testament of the Bible, and it is thought they were the first people to learn to navigate by the North Star.

Other nations thought so highly of the Phoenicians' seamanship that they hired their sailors and bought their ships. As well as supplying King Solomon of Israel with help on a long-distance sea journey in about 950 B.C., it is believed the Phoenicians may have made an incredible 21,700-mile journey around Africa, on behalf of King Necho II of Egypt, in 600 B.C. At that time, no one had any idea of the enormous size of Africa. The expedition is believed to have set off into completely unknown waters and taken three years to complete. The story may be true because it was reported by the travelers that they saw the sun in the northern sky. From the southern hemisphere the sun appears to rise in the east and pass in the northern sky to set in the west. So this report could mean they did travel south of the equator.

**Above** The Phoenicians were not only great sailors and explorers but also skilled at crafts. This ivory carving shows a man being killed by a lioness.

**Around Africa**
Whether the Phoenicians sailed all the way around Africa in 600 B.C. is an unsolved mystery of exploration. Our only source of information is the Greek historian Herodotus, who wrote, "We know that it [Africa] is washed on all sides by the sea except where it joins Asia, as was first demonstrated…by Necho, the Egyptian King, who…sent out a fleet manned by a Phoenician crew with orders to sail from the Arabian Gulf and return to Egypt by way of the Straits of Gibraltar."

The Phoenicians set up colonies all over the Mediterranean where there were good harbors and watering places along their trade routes. One such Phoenician colony in the western Mediterranean was Carthage, which became a city and trading center of fabulous wealth and luxury.

It was from there the Carthaginians traveled beyond the Mediterranean. They sailed out and found islands such as the Canary Islands in the Atlantic Ocean and explored parts of the coast of Africa. They set up a base at Gades, (now called Cádiz) on the Atlantic coast to control trade in this area.

At about the same time that Hanno and his colonists from Carthage made their journey around the northwest coast of Africa, an expedition from Gades under a commander called Himilco set sail to search for the fabled Tin Islands, said to be in the North Atlantic. Tin was valuable to the Mediterranean people for making bronze. Himilco was away for about four months. He probably followed the coast of Spain and France, and some believe he may even have landed in Cornwall, in England.

The records we have about the Phoenicians and Carthaginians are very unreliable. For one thing they were jealous and secretive about their trading routes – they even sank one of their ships rather than let a Roman competitor know where it was going. Also, any records the Phoenicians did keep were destroyed by conquering civilizations. Most of what we know is secondhand, written by Greek historians at a later date.

**Below** An artist's impression of the impressive seaport colony of Carthage.

CARTHAGE HARBOR (450 B.C.)

Mediterranean Sea

Outer harbor

Inner harbor

# Viking colonists and traders

From the shores of Scandinavia, the Vikings launched their longboats into rough seas, guided only by frightening stories of the possible dangers. People believed that the earth was flat, so they might fall off the edge if they went too far – or else sea monsters would rise from the ocean depths to attack them.

No one had ventured out across the Atlantic Ocean before, because without compasses and maps, sailors needed to stay within sight of land. In A.D. 1000, Leif Eriksson and a crew of thirty bravely sailed an open boat west across the wild north Atlantic Ocean, where the waves could reach a height of 100 feet. In the cramped, wet, and cold conditions on the longboat, the crew huddled in their leather sleeping bags in the bottom of the boat when there was time to rest. It would have been several

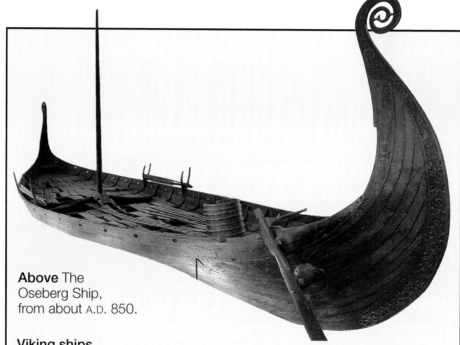

**Above** The Oseberg Ship, from about A.D. 850.

### Viking ships

A Viking ship was usually about 65 – 100 feet long and had a woolen sail, often striped blue and white or red and white. The boat could also be rowed. It was clinker-built (made from overlapping planks of wood nailed together), the joints stuffed with moss, hair, or rope to make them watertight. The solid oak keel was like a strong backbone supporting the mast and a single sail. The prow was decorated with a fierce carving, often a dragon or snake head.

weeks before they reached land. We now know that they landed in North America, probably on Newfoundland, Canada. They found a pleasant country with wheat and grapes and rivers rich in salmon.

Leif returned home and encouraged Viking settlers to make the difficult journey to Vinland, as they called it. But after three years the colony failed. Vinland was abandoned and forgotten.

It would be almost five hundred years before anyone else managed to cross the Atlantic Ocean – and return to tell the tale!

GREENLAND
ICELAND
SCANDINAVIA
RUSSIA
NORTH
AMERICA
Vinland
(Newfoundland)
IRELAND  ENGLAND
Mediterranean
Sea
Atlantic Ocean
NORTH AFRICA

- - - - Leif Eriksson's further exploration of North America
——— Leif Eriksson's route to Vinland
——— Viking voyages

### Erik finds Greenland

Erik the Red, the father of Leif Eriksson, was banished from Iceland in A.D. 982 for committing a murder. He sailed out into the Atlantic, hoping that a rumor he had heard of an island to the west was true. After a long and difficult journey, he found an island he later called Greenland.

In about A.D. 986 others decided to join him and twenty-five ships set sail from Iceland, each carrying twenty to twenty-five people, livestock, household goods, and tools. On the two-week voyage, the angry seas swept away all but fourteen ships. The survivors reached Greenland and set up two colonies. But the harsh climate and lack of good land and trees to build shelter and provide heat prevented the colonies from flourishing. They had disappeared by the sixteenth century.

The Viking sailor Leif Eriksson in Vinland, which is thought to have been Newfoundland, Canada. One of the first tasks for Leif Eriksson and his crew would have been to chop down trees to build an encampment.

## Viking colonists and traders

Although the Vikings were brave explorers, they were also raiders and plunderers. The first expeditions from their homelands of Denmark, Norway, and Sweden (known as Scandinavia) in A.D. 793 were to attack settlements in countries close by, such as England and France, stealing whatever they could carry back to their ships.

**Below** The Vikings were not only great explorers but also fierce warriors. This stone carving shows a Viking warrior on horseback.

They began to explore outside Scandinavia for two reasons: good farm land was scarce in parts of Scandinavia and often, as in the case of Erik the Red's banishment, there were wars or troubles at home that meant they had to find a new place to live. With their great skill as sailors, the Norwegian Vikings reached Iceland and later Greenland and North America.

In the open sea, the Vikings were fearless navigators. Without maps or compasses to guide them, they could keep track of their position only by the sun and stars. The Vikings may have had "sunstones." These were crystals that would show where the sun was, even in an overcast sky. Out at sea, sighting sea gulls or seaweed sometimes showed that land was close by. By skill and guesswork they calculated their approximate position.

Like the Phoenicians, their skill in boat building

### Raid
"Never before has such terror appeared in Britain as we have now suffered from the pagan race; nor was it thought that such an attack could have been made from the sea." (Northumbrian priest, Alcuin, Great Britain, after a Viking attack on Holy Island [or Lindisfarne], June A.D. 793.)

### Sagas
The Vikings were poets and storytellers, which is partly why we know what they did. Their sagas were long tales of heroes, warriors, and exploration. These were passed from generation to generation by word of mouth until the thirteenth century, when they were first written down.

### Viking traders
All along the routes of the Dneiper and Volga rivers (in present-day Russia), the Vikings set up a network of trading posts, and in some places they settled. In one area the people called the newcomers the "Rus" – the name Russia comes from this word. The Arab traveler Ibn Fadlan described them, saying each one was tall, blond-haired and covered in tattoos "from his fingernails to his neck."

Furs

Walrus ivory

**Above** Viking traders presenting furs and ivory to the Byzantine court.

was one of the reasons the Vikings were able to travel so far. The boat they used most was the longship, a canoe-shaped warship that was tough enough to sail through heavy seas; but on their longer journeys they usually sailed in a more solid boat called the knorr. It was broader and could carry a large amount of cargo and more people.

Trade, too, was a reason for Viking explorations. The Swedish Vikings set out in the opposite direction of the Norwegians, sailing east along rivers into the heart of Europe. Where they reached the head of a river or an impassable stretch of water, they either carried their boats or dragged them overland to the next river or lake.

The rivers led the Vikings to the Caspian Sea and trade with the ancient Persians, as well as to Constantinople (now Istanbul in Turkey) one of the great international trading centers of the time. The Byzantine emperor who ruled the city was impressed with their strength and made some of the Vikings his bodyguards. They became known as the Varangian Guard.

In Constantinople, merchants from all over the known world gathered: Arabs, Chinese, Indians, Europeans, and many more. The Vikings offered wax, rope, honey, timber, walrus ivory, and furs for sale. In return they sought precious stones, gold and silver, china, glass, and silks. The Viking boats also brought slaves for trading in Constantinople, in particular captured Slav peasants. These were the unfortunate people who gave us the word "slave."

# Learned Arab travelers

A Moroccan named Ibn Battuta left his home on June 14, 1325. He was a devout Muslim and wanted to make a pilgrimage to Mecca, the holy Muslim city. He did not return home for almost thirty years, having covered at least 75,000 miles.

Ibn Battuta found he enjoyed traveling, and after beginning his journeys in the Middle East, he toured down the east coast of Africa. He decided early never to follow the same road twice. Heading north, he tried to travel to the "Land of Darkness" – Siberia – but he ran out of supplies.

He made his way east to India and was welcomed by the Sultan of Delhi, who employed him for a while. When Ibn Battuta set off from Delhi for China, he had a narrow escape. Not far from the city he was attacked by Hindu rebels, captured, and nearly executed. They took all his belongings except his clothes. He returned to India, and later sailed to Sumatra, where the ruler lent Ibn Battuta a boat that finally landed him in China. He was very impressed by the things he saw there, such as the black stone that the Chinese burned as fuel (coal) and beautiful porcelain.

## Caravan

During the Middle Ages, the most common way to travel long distances was to join a caravan. Travelers faced dangers from bandits, and the caravan offered safety. Ibn Battuta described a pilgrim caravan he traveled with in 1326. He said that there were so many people "that the earth surged with them like the sea … the caravan included busy bazaars and all sorts of food and fruit. They used to march at night and light torches in front of the files of camels … so that you saw the country gleaming with light.…"

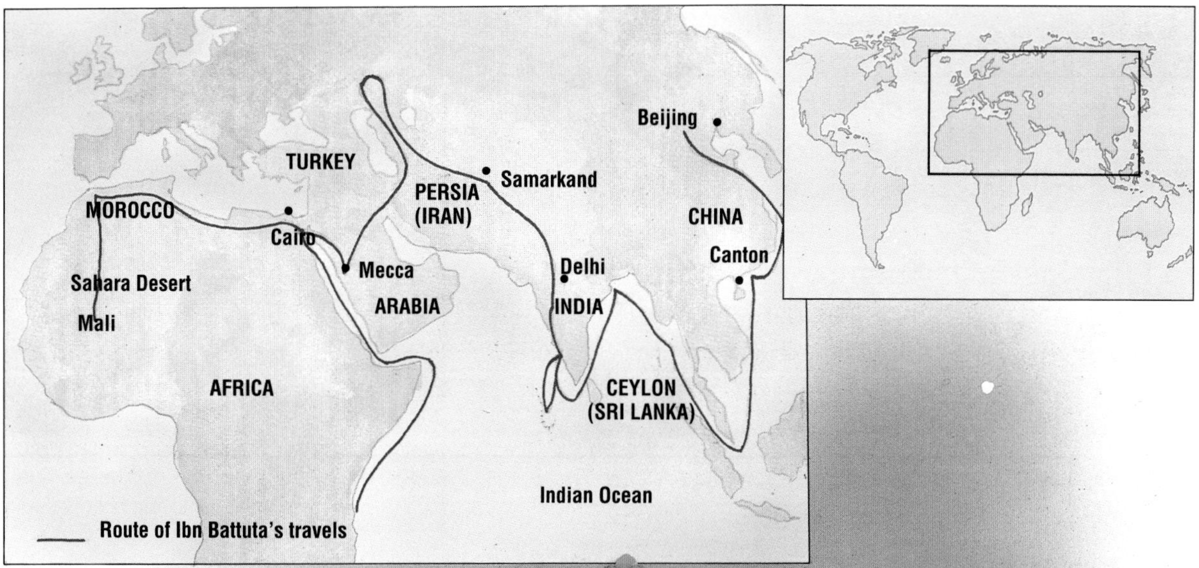
Beijing
TURKEY
Samarkand
PERSIA
(IRAN)
MOROCCO
CHINA
Cairo
Canton
Mecca
Delhi
Sahara Desert
ARABIA
INDIA
Mali
AFRICA
CEYLON
(SRI LANKA)
Indian Ocean
Route of Ibn Battuta's travels

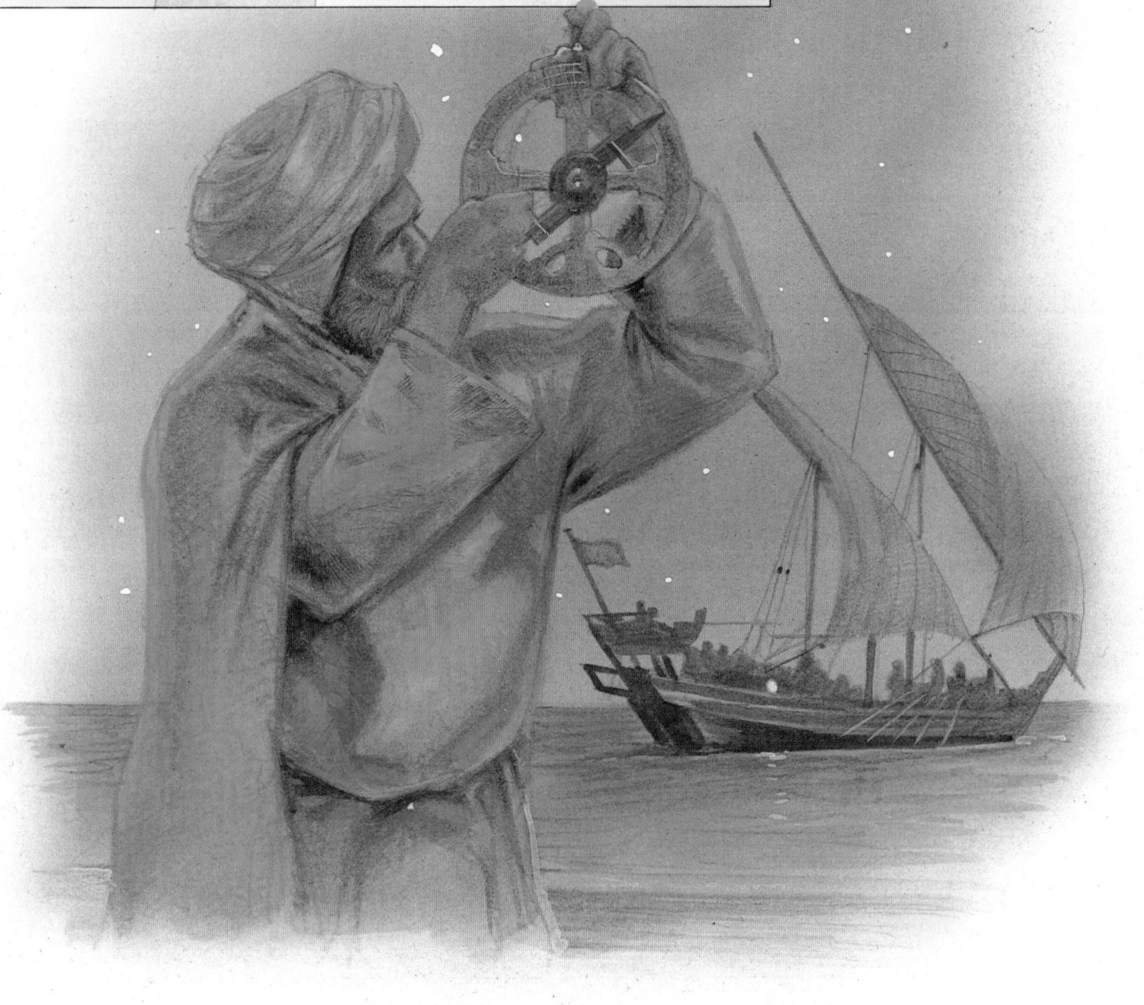

An Arab navigator using an astrolabe, an instrument originally developed by the Greeks for measuring sun and star altitudes. The Arabs used it to calculate the position of seaports.

Ibn Battuta's travels were special because he was the only traveler of his era who we know visited every Muslim country, as well as many others – sixty rulers in all. Muslims had been traveling and exploring since the middle of the eighth century. Some, like Ibn Battuta, were inspired by their religion to visit other Muslim countries, but most were merchants seeking new markets for trade.

Soon after the Arabs became Muslim (in the seventh century A.D.), they began to conquer lands around them. When they had established themselves in the Middle East and north and east Africa, their travels took them farther east. At its greatest extent the Arab Muslim empire reached from Spain to China.

One result was a boom in trade from east to west, with new and old routes opening up. By the ninth century A.D. about 150,000 foreign traders, mostly Muslims, lived in Canton in China. Merchants traveled overland by caravan or by sea across the Indian Ocean.

Although the Arabs had always been seafarers, their knowledge and skill grew during this time, making them some of the most experienced navigators in the world. Not only did they have instruments such as the astrolabe, but they produced rahmani, texts that contained such information as details about ports, wind directions, reefs, and tides.

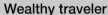

**Wealthy traveler**
Ibn Battuta was an educated man from a rich family, and he usually sought out important people to help him as he traveled. He met and stayed with princes and rulers, often giving and receiving lavish gifts. He described the Sultan of Delhi: "This king is of all men the fondest of making gifts and shedding blood. His gate is never without some poor man enriched or some living man executed."

**Left** This painting from about 1237 shows rich Muslims traveling in a caravan with camels and horses. For centuries Muslims have crossed enormous distances to visit the holy city of Mecca.

In Europe it was the Dark Ages, but Islamic culture had been flourishing from A.D. 750, under the great Abbasid dynasty in its capital at Baghdad (in present-day Iraq). In science, geography, and mathematics the Arabs used and expanded ideas from the earlier Indian, Persian, and Greek civilizations. For example, Ptolemy's famous book *Geography*, which had been written in the second century A.D., was well-known to the Arabs.

The Arabs were seekers of knowledge and, following the merchants, educated geographers and explorers set out to find out about and record the Islamic and non-Islamic world. One such Muslim traveler was Ibn Fadlan, who was sent in A.D. 921 from Baghdad to Russia on a mission to the Bulgar court. Here he met the Rus people, Viking settlers whom he described as dirty and primitive.

With their skills and learning, the Arabs came to write many carefully researched geography books, with details about the customs and lives of people of other lands. Al-Idrisi was one of their most famous geographers.

This painting shows the type of Arab boat that would have been used by Ibn Battuta to sail in the Persian Gulf.

**Travel stories**
Nearly all the great Arab travelers wrote books about the people and places they visited. Ibn Battuta's book has many details about religions and customs because he was a very devout Muslim. He also describes the kind of goods for sale in markets and what was grown in the countryside. Writing about Tabriz in Persia (now Iran), he said: "Here there is a fine hospice, where travelers are supplied with food, consisting of bread, meat, rice cooked in butter, and sweetmeats…we came to a great bazaar…one of the finest bazaars I have seen the world over…my eyes were dazzled by the precious stones that I beheld."

He traveled widely in Europe and parts of Asia, and went to stay at the court of the Christian king, Roger II of Sicily.

Al-Idrisi wrote a book for Roger II in 1154 called *The Stroll of One Wishing to Traverse the Horizons of the Globe*. It gives details of the culture and economic life of all the known countries of Asia, Europe, and Africa.

# A glimpse of the East

Few Europeans had seen the Far East in 1271. The journey, whether by land or by sea, was long and full of dangers. There was no certainty, either, of warm welcome. One Italian traveler, Marco Polo, had a good introduction: his father and uncle had already been there and met Kublai Khan, the Mongol ruler of China.

The Polos were merchants from Venice, which was one of the busiest European trading ports in the late Middle Ages. In 1271 they began their second journey east, taking the young Marco with them. He was seventeen years old.

It took them three and a half years to get to China. As well as having to cross bandit-ridden country, they fell sick along the way. The Polos struggled through the snow of the highest mountains of Asia and skirted south of the wastes of the Gobi desert. Marco told of "spirit voices" in the desert

**Above** Marco Polo arriving in Hormuz in the Persian Gulf.

talking to the travelers, luring them away from the correct path.

When they reached China, Kublai Khan gave young Marco Polo a job as an official. For nearly twenty years he traveled around China and its neighboring countries, working for the Khan and learning about the strange lands and their peoples.

**The Silk Road**

Marco Polo journeyed to China along the Silk Road, a route from Europe that had been used by merchants for hundreds of years to bring goods, such as the much sought-after silk, from China. Few merchants traveled the whole route, but traded goods with others at well-known markets along the way, such as Samarkand and Constantinople.

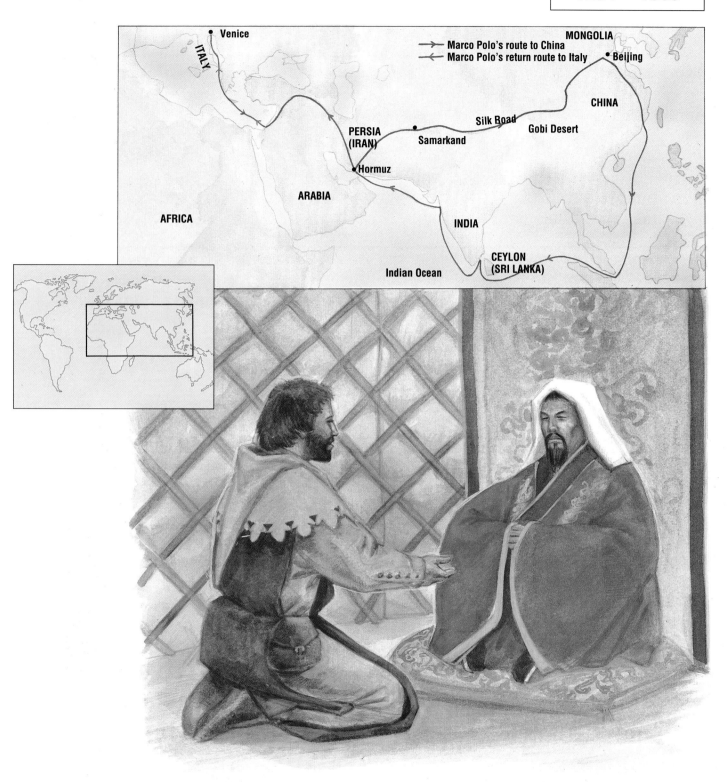

After traveling thousands of miles overland, Marco Polo reached China and met the ruler, Kublai Khan.

The Polos' travels took place during a period of peace after the onslaught by the most powerful conqueror the world has ever seen, Genghis Khan. In the early part of the thirteenth century his ferocious army of tribesmen from the open plains of Mongolia swept across large parts of China, Asia, and the Middle East, stopping on the fringes of Europe.

Lands under Mongol rule gradually became more settled, and trade flourished across their huge empire. Genghis Khan's grandson, Kublai Khan, set up a capital at Beijing in China. He was tolerant of other religions and peoples, and his court became busy with foreigners from many different countries.

Kublai Khan adopted some of the ways and life-style of the great Chinese civilization that had existed for several centuries before the Mongol invasion. In many ways China's society and culture were ahead of the west at that time.

Scientific inventions (which were not to reach Europe until later) were already in use; for example, the compass, gunpowder, and devices to measure earthquakes. The Chinese had also invented water clocks to tell time. Marco Polo was impressed by the enormous size of Chinese cities and the markets full of goods from foreign countries. He described with surprise how the Chinese used paper money, for in Europe only metal coins were used.

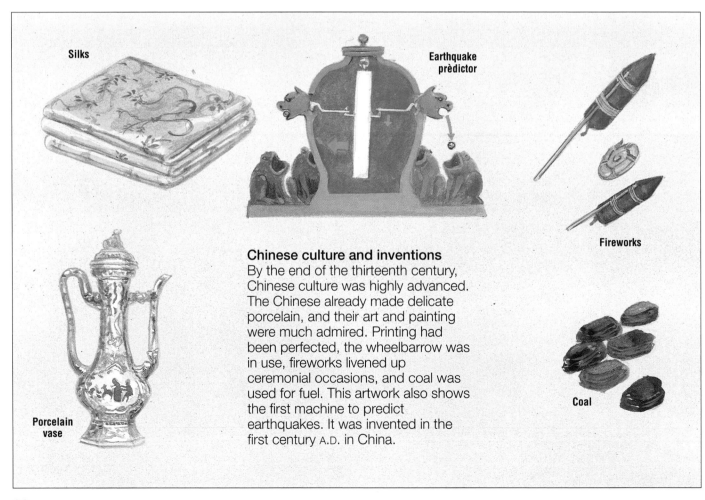

**Silks**

**Earthquake prèdictor**

**Fireworks**

**Porcelain vase**

**Coal**

**Chinese culture and inventions**
By the end of the thirteenth century, Chinese culture was highly advanced. The Chinese already made delicate porcelain, and their art and painting were much admired. Printing had been perfected, the wheelbarrow was in use, fireworks livened up ceremonial occasions, and coal was used for fuel. This artwork also shows the first machine to predict earthquakes. It was invented in the first century A.D. in China.

Other European travelers were also making the journey to China. Although at first scared of the Mongol tribes, some Europeans saw them as possible allies against the Muslims, with whom Christian Europe was at war. A number of missionaries were sent to try to convert the Mongols to Christianity.

One such person was John of Monte Corvino, from Italy, who made the long and difficult journey to Beijing in 1292, bearing a letter from the Pope to Kublai Khan. He remained in China until he died in 1328, and set up several Christian communities,

**Above** A book of Marco Polo's travels shows the type of Chinese junks used by Marco Polo when he visited nearby islands and countries while working for Kublai Khan.

although he never managed to convert the Mongols.

These travelers were lucky to get a glimpse of the great Chinese civilization – many of the places they visited were not seen again by Europeans until the nineteenth century. Soon after the Polos left, overland routes to China were closed because of wars, and then, after the fall of the foreign Mongol rulers in 1368, China shut her borders to outsiders.

Marco Polo's book about his travels was treated with disbelief by many people in Europe. They had very little knowledge about the rest of the world, and thought Polo's stories too far-fetched to be true. But gradually his tale became accepted and it was realized there were

great riches to be found in the East. The book became a source of inspiration to geographers, mapmakers, and later explorers, such as Christopher Columbus.

**Chinese exploration**
Between 1405 and 1433, the Chinese went on a series of expeditions. The Chinese emperor sent a commander called Zheng He out with a fleet of junks (Chinese sailboats) that reached other countries in the Far East, India, and even the east coast of Africa.

The boats carried diplomats, translators, merchants, and doctors who tried to keep people healthy on board by growing fresh vegetables on deck.

On returning home, Zheng He caused quite a stir in the Chinese court with the giraffes, lions, and ostriches he presented to the emperor.

**Strange creature**
Reading this description by Marco Polo of an animal he saw, you might agree that his stories were a bit difficult to believe: "There are some of them ten paces in length… They have two squat legs in front near the head, which have no feet but simply three claws …They have enormous heads and eyes so bulging that they are bigger than loaves. Their mouth is big enough to swallow a man at one gulp. Their teeth are huge." It is something we all now know about. What was it? A crocodile, of course!

# The scramble for riches

Explorers have also been plunderers and conquerors. The rich Inca civilization had survived high in the Andes mountains of Peru for over 300 years. Then in 1531 the Spanish landed on the coast of South America and started inland, searching for the Inca's fabled cities and their gold.

Leading the Spanish was Francisco Pizarro, a man of humble origins whose aim in life was to become rich and famous. His expedition had well-trained men, modern weapons, and horses. Even so, it was tough traveling thousands of miles from home in a hostile country. When the men wanted to give up, Pizarro said, "Let none of you lose heart…God fights for us. He will humble the pride of these heathen and bring them to the true faith."

After crossing deserts, the Spanish had a long climb up into the Andes. They faced danger from the defending Incas, and disease spread; men and horses struggled for breath at the high altitudes. A Spanish historian of the time told how "no clothes or armor were sufficient to keep out the icy wind that pierced and froze them."

**Inca civilization**
The Inca civilization was rich in gold and highly organized. A Spaniard described their city of Cuzco as "so beautiful and has such fine buildings that it would be remarkable even in Spain." When Francisco Pizarro and his soldiers first saw the Inca ruler, Atahualpa, and his huge army, the Spanish gasped at the gold and jewels worn by the Inca and at Atahualpa's litter that shone "like the sun."

**Right** A gold ceremonial knife from Peru, dating from the twelfth or thirteenth century.

Puna
Island

Tumbers

Paita

PERU

Cajamarca

Pacific Ocean

A n d e s   M o u n t a i n s

Cuzco

—— Francisco Pizarro's route

Francisco Pizarro led his soldiers through the Andes mountains in search of the legendary gold of the Incas.

## Inca defeat

Francisco Pizarro led 180 Spanish soldiers through the Andes to the town of Cajamarca. Here, they met with Atahualpa and his army of 30,000. Pizarro said "The men were full of fear for we were so deep in a land where we could not be reinforced."

Atahualpa agreed to meet with Pizarro but when he refused to surrender to the Spanish, he was taken prisoner. Pizarro noted that Atahualpa "was quick to learn our ways…even to learn the language of Spain. We found ourselves liking this man." However, the Spaniards killed Atahualpa when he rejected the Bible.

**Above** Vasco da Gama handing the ruler of Calicut, in India, a letter from the King of Portugal.

From the early fifteenth century, Europeans set out on a series of brave and remarkable journeys of exploration. The chance of new trade and greed for easily found wealth pushed them to break the boundaries known at that time.

At the forefront were the Portuguese, searching for new sea routes to the Far East when wars blocked overland trade. In 1497 and 1498, Vasco da Gama sailed around Africa and reached India by sea. During the early sixteenth century, Portuguese ships finally discovered a route to the east. They took control of much of Europe's trade with countries in the Far East,

trade that had been previously in the hands of the Arab explorers.

Sailing these huge distances was often a terrifying adventure. Even though Europeans now knew the world was round, the explorers had very little idea as to its size and what lands lay where. As well as the

dangers of shipwreck in uncharted seas, there was the threat of pirates, who infested many coasts such as those around India and Malaysia.

While the Portuguese were exploring to the east, the Spanish were sailing west. Christopher Columbus persuaded the Spanish to back his trip to explore a new route across the Atlantic Ocean. In 1492, after a historic and brave journey, he landed on a Caribbean island. He believed he had found islands in the Far East.

The Spanish occupied the Caribbean islands; the native population were either turned into slaves or died from diseases brought by the Europeans. Exploring further, the Spanish reached the mainland of North America with their imaginations fired with stories of gold. It was in Peru and Mexico that they found it; in the same way that Pizarro had defeated

---

**Destruction of a race**
Columbus had hoped to find gold in the Caribbean islands. When he did not he turned to slaving, shipping the Carib people of the islands to Spain for sale. Others were forced to work for the Spanish, and many died from disease or overwork. Las Casas, a priest, said that the system was "abominable." On the island of Hispaniola, the population was 300,000 in 1492; fifteen years later, only some 60,000 native people were left. Thirty years later there was virtually none.

the Incas, in Mexico the Spaniard Hernando Cortés destroyed and plundered the great Aztec civilization. Although the Spanish explored parts of North America too, these expeditions were considered a failure, for they found no gold.

As well as the search for riches, the conquistadores (conquerors) of the Americas had another reason for being there. They hoped to convert the people to Christianity. So priests were taken on the journeys, some of whom were as cruel as the conquistadores themselves in their treatment of the native people.

**Above** This painting shows a priest urging Pizarro's men to fight the Incas.

The British, Dutch, and French followed the Spanish and Portuguese explorers. To start with, they had found it worthwhile capturing Spanish ships returning with gold from the New World. Later, they too set out on voyages to explore and settle the huge continent of North America and the Caribbean islands on the far side of the Atlantic.

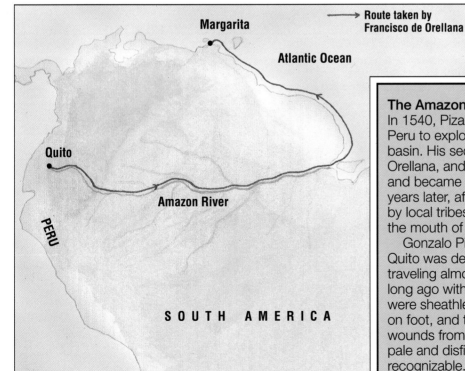

**The Amazon basin**

In 1540, Pizarro's half brother Gonzalo set out from Peru to explore the Quito region in the Amazon basin. His second-in-command, Francisco de Orellana, and about fifty men were sent on ahead and became separated from the main group. Two years later, after nearly starving and being attacked by local tribesmen, Orellana and his men reached the mouth of the Amazon.

Gonzalo Pizarro had turned back; his return to Quito was described as follows: "They were traveling almost naked, for their clothes had rotted long ago with the continual rains…Their swords were sheathless and eaten with rust. They were all on foot, and their arms and legs were scarred with wounds from the thorns and bushes. They were so pale and disfigured that they were scarcely recognizable."

# The Pacific explored

One-third of the world's surface is covered by the Pacific Ocean, and in 1768 only a tiny part of it had been explored. Although there were others before and after, the most important discoveries were made by Captain James Cook, who set out that year, in the *Endeavour*, on his first journey into the uncharted Pacific Ocean.

In three voyages over a period of eleven years he sailed thousands of miles from his native England, reaching islands such as Tahiti, Easter Island, Christmas Island, and Hawaii. He mapped the coast of New Zealand in 1769 and in 1770 was the first European to land on and chart the east coast of what later became known as Australia. This voyage and his other journeys also took him into the Southern Ocean.

Cook tried out new boats, navigational instruments, and new ways to keep men healthy on long sea expeditions. His

**Above** Cook's ships, *Resolution* and *Adventure*, land at Tahiti in 1773.

### On board
Although on his first trip he sailed with just one ship, Cook preferred to have two – the other could always help when there was trouble. Each carried around 100 people, including one or two scientists or artists.

boats were built especially to withstand running aground. He insisted that his men eat vegetables and fresh food when possible, for in those days one in three men who set sail in the British fleet died, mostly from the disease scurvy.

### Healthy cabbage
The sailors could be at sea for more than one hundred days without seeing land or fresh food. Cook insisted that his men eat sauerkraut (pickled cabbage) regularly to help prevent scurvy. But it was difficult to persuade them to eat the cabbage: "Such are the tempers and dispositions of Seamen in general that whatever you give them out of the Common Way, altho' it be ever so much for their good yet it will not go down." So Cook made sure the sailors saw his officers eating it and "the Moment they see their Superiors set a Value upon it, it becomes the finest stuff in the World." He had to ration his men after that because they ate so much!

Voyages of Captain James Cook
1768-1771 First Voyage
1772-1775 Second Voyage
1776-1779 Third Voyage

BRITAIN

AFRICA

CHINA

INDIA

Indian Ocean

AUSTRALIA

NEW ZEALAND

ANTARCTIC

Pacific Ocean

Tahiti

Friendly Islands

Alaska

CANADA

NORTH AMERICA

Atlantic Ocean

Hawaiian Islands

SOUTH AMERICA

Captain James Cook using a sextant to measure his ship's latitude. Cook was an experienced sailor who, by the age of 40, had sailed on many different ships. He surveyed the rivers and coastline of Canada before his adventures in the Pacific Ocean.

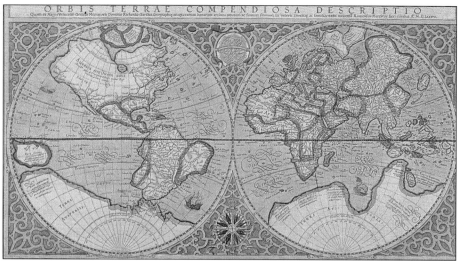

The Pacific Ocean had been discovered some 250 years before by Ferdinand Magellan, but why was it that no one had explored it thoroughly? Europeans at the time imagined the Pacific to be a vast ocean without any lands with gold or other riches – which was a major reason for their explorations in other parts of the world. It was just an obstacle to be crossed to reach the spice-rich islands of the Far East.

However, for a long time there had been a rumor that a southern continent existed, called "*Terra Australis*." This was thought to lie south and probably east of Australia, and was believed to be an island, although it had not been mapped. We now know that the landmass is the vast ice-covered continent of Antarctica.

European countries such as England, France, Spain, and Portugal had been acquiring land all over the world during the previous two hundred years, each country competing against the other for power and control. Some had made halfhearted attempts to explore the Pacific, but it was England that decided to mount an expedition to search for the legendary *Terra Australis*. James Cook was instructed on his first journey to find this land (which he never reached) and claim it for England.

Cook's journeys marked a turning point in the history of exploration: by the time he finished, the inhabited world had been mapped in outline terms. The great improvements in equipment and navigation (such as the invention of the chronometer) were also important in making sea exploration less hazardous and uncertain.

### A skilled mapmaker

Cook mapped every place he visited very carefully. A French officer sailing around New Zealand a few years later said that Cook's map was "of an exactitude and of a thoroughness of detail which astonished me beyond all power of expression. I doubt whether our own coasts of France have been delineated [drawn] with more precision."

### The marine chronometer

By 1762, sailors could make a fairly good calculation about latitude (their north-south position) using the marine sextant. Longitude (east–west position) was more difficult to work out. What was needed was an accurate timepiece so that the distance traveled from a known place could be calculated. John Harrison developed a chronometer in 1762, and Cook tested it on his voyages. It became a standard piece of navigational equipment.

During this period a new interest in exploration appeared – scientific investigation. On board his ship, Cook not only had sailors but also scientists, who studied the plants and animals of lands they found, and artists, who recorded what they saw, drawing pictures of people, plants, and places.

James Cook and these new scientific explorers who traveled with him were generally friendly with the native people they met. The European outsiders were there to study rather than to conquer.

Cook himself drew up rules for his crew for behavior with local people. His first rule was "To endeavour by every fair means to cultivate a friendship with the natives and to treat them with all imaginable humanity."

To the islanders, European men must have seemed like aliens from outer space. Cook usually tried exchanging presents first. The most popular gift was nails, since the islanders had no metals at all; the Europeans requested fresh supplies such as water and fruit in exchange. Quite often the native people welcomed the Europeans, entertaining them with singing and dancing. For the sailors, the Pacific islands were like paradise, and Cook used to have great trouble persuading his men to leave.

**Friendly islanders**

In his diary Cook wrote in detail about his discoveries and the people he met. Usually he got along well with the native people of the islands he visited. In October 1773 he wrote, "At 8 o'Clock we discovered a small Island …after we had come to Anchor, I went a Shore with Captain Furneaux…we were welcomed …[by] …an immense crowd of Men and Women …with Cloth, Matting, etc. to exchange for Nails…at last the Chief cleared the way…to his house which was situated in a most delightful spot…I ordered the bagpipes to be played and in return the Chief ordered three young women to Sing."

**Above** This drawing shows Captain Cook and his men being met by islanders with gifts of fruit as they land on the island of Middleburgh.

# The new frontier

In 1783 England recognized the independence of its thirteen American colonies, which became known as the United States of America. The new country consisted only of a strip of land along the east coast of North America; beyond was a huge land, mostly unexplored by European settlers. A few French explorers and fur trappers, who had traveled down from Canada, were the only Europeans who had any idea of what lay to the west.

The great Mississippi River was the chief waterway of these unknown lands, and it lay within the French territory of Louisiana. (The map opposite shows what a huge area this covered.) The third president of the U.S., Thomas Jefferson, arranged in 1803 to buy Louisiana from the French. For the sum of fifteen million dollars, the size of the U.S. was doubled.

Jefferson wanted to find out what he had bought, so he appointed two men to lead an exploratory expedition. The leaders, Meriwether Lewis and William Clark, were both experienced at living in the wild. In May 1804 they set off with forty-five men, intending to explore Louisiana and discover a land route to the Pacific Ocean.

**Above** A painting of Lewis and Clark on the Columbia River during their expedition to explore the uncharted west of North America (1804–1806).

**Wet Pacific**
When Lewis and Clark reached the Pacific Ocean there was no chance of celebrating, "for winter was upon the men…Lewis and Clark established quarters in a crudely constructed, flea-ridden stockade they called Fort Clatsop…it was burdened with endless coastal rains and bitter, cold weather. Only six days of sunshine lifted the men's spirits between January and late March."

**Sacajawea**

On their expedition across North America, Lewis and Clark were guided by Sacajawea, a Shoshoni Indian. She knew some of the many different languages of the native peoples and some of the passes through the mountains. Once when the expedition boat capsized on the Missouri River, she sat calmly on the upturned stern and rescued as much of their equipment as she could when it floated past.

Pacific Ocean

New York

USA (BEFORE 1803)

Washington DC

Atlantic Ocean

— LOUISIANA LAND PURCHASE AREA
→ Route taken by Lewis and Clark

Sacajawea helping Lewis and Clark to find a trail through the Rocky Mountains. She was only sixteen years old when she and her husband joined the expedition in the area of North Dakota – and she was pregnant.

Out in the wilds of the American west, Lewis and Clark and their party faced endless dangers and difficulties. On the first stage of their journey they were troubled by mosquitoes and gnats, as well as by stomach upsets. They had to build their own boats and then carts to take their belongings around the Great Falls of the Missouri River. In the Rocky Mountains, they were constantly troubled by bears. After canoeing down the Columbia River, they finally reached the Pacific Ocean.

The expedition members recorded everything new that they found. In particular they collected information on soil, animals, and plants and made maps of the areas they passed through. Their reports included information on furs, which encouraged trappers such as Jedediah Smith to explore the area further.

Jefferson had given Lewis and Clark strict instructions to make friends with any native peoples they met. It helped that they had a guide, named Sacajawea, and that when the Shoshoni of Idaho became hostile, she turned out to be the chief's sister. The expedition was low on stores and she persuaded the local people to supply food, horses, and guides for the difficult crossing of the Rocky Mountains.

After wintering by the Pacific Ocean, Lewis and Clark returned home overland, exploring new country. On the way they met a team of trappers, known as the "Mountain Men," who had already begun to use one of the routes the expedition had marked out. These signposted rough trails became the highways both

**Right** A painting from 1844 called *The Trapper* shows a typical "Mountain Man" of the time.

### Jedediah Smith

One Mountain Man was Jedediah Smith, known as the "knight in buckskin" to his friends. He was slightly unusual because he did not smoke or chew tobacco or drink much, unlike most other fur trappers.

During nine years of exploration and trapping from 1822 to 1831, he traveled more than 15,500 miles, finding new trails in the remote west.

for the Mountain Men and for other organized expeditions that followed. From the maps and information these later explorers took back to the east, official routes were planned and trails built. Not long after, settlers started to pour across North America.

In the middle of winter in the isolated mountains of western North America, fur traders were exploring new trails. The coldest part of the year was the prime hunting season, when the beavers' valuable coats were thickest.

There were not many of these tough Mountain Men. They were independent, strong, and hardy because they had to cross deep snow, icy water, and harsh mountains, as well as face hostile Native Americans and the occasional grizzly bear. Carrying a rifle, pistol, tomahawk, scalping knife, and a bag of "possibles" or odds and ends, they roved singly or in small groups, exploring trails from the Mississippi Valley to the Rocky Mountains, and from Canada to Arizona.

Every year at the spring meetings, trappers gathered to trade the season's pelts to the big fur companies. Caravans brought goods and supplies to sell to the trappers, who also collected newspapers and letters. The meeting, called a *rendezvous*, had a festive atmosphere and was a break from their usual hard, lonely life in the wilds.

### Opening trails

The days of the fur-trapping Mountain Men were soon over: by the 1830s the number of beavers had rapidly declined and the demand for furs was beginning to fall. However, the trails the Mountain Men had blazed opened new areas for settlers, and some trappers were able to become guides for the rush of people moving west.

**Above** This painting, entitled *Watching the Wagons*, shows Native Americans watching white settlers in a wagon train crossing their traditional homeland.

# The Victorian in Africa

In 1895 a white English woman was being paddled in a canoe up the Ogowe River in West Africa. Her name was Mary Kingsley. She was on her second trip to a part of the world known as the "White Man's Grave," so called because so many European travelers had died there from tropical diseases and accidents. People who knew her thought she was crazy to go exploring there, but when her parents died she decided to study African religion and law so that she could finish a book her father had begun to write.

Her canoe was full of things considered essential to the Victorian explorer – her books and papers, photographic materials, an insect collecting case, a mosquito net to sleep under, clothes, and a chest of medicines. She also carried goods to sell, such as tobacco and fish hooks.

Mary Kingsley had spent five months studying the people and collecting insects and fish in the swamps and river mouths along the coast of West Africa. She then wanted to go inland for several more months to experience unexplored Africa. Five local men accompanied her, but she had no other traveling companions.

On her way upriver she traded at riverside villages and with the fearsome Fang tribe. Being naturally curious, Kingsley would try all the local foods (such as snake), and she had no fears about tramping through the forest with the local people. She later described her experiences in lively books about West Africa.

**Suitable clothes**

Mary Kingsley usually wore a white blouse and a long black skirt. As she said, "One should not go about Africa in something of which one would be ashamed at home." Underneath she sometimes wore a pair of her brother's old trousers, which at least protected her from leeches found in the swamps she crossed. Once she fell into an elephant trap and later wrote, "It is at times like these you realize the blessing of a good thick skirt." The many layers of cloth and petticoats prevented any spikes from getting through.

**Cannibals**

The Fang people of West Africa lived by farming in the forest clearings and by hunting and fishing. They collected ivory from elephants' tusks and rubber for trading. The Fang were also cannibals. Mary Kingsley stayed in a chief's house one night and found a bag hanging on the wall. Inside she found "bits and pieces of humanity – eyes, ears, toes and the like." Kingsley wrote, "I subsequently learned that although the Fan[g] will eat their fellow friendly tribes-folk, yet they like to keep a little momento."

AFRICA

Freetown
Accra
Calabra
Atlantic Ocean
St. Paul de
Loanda
Indian Ocean

—— Route of Mary Kingsley's travels 1893-1895

Mary Kingsley was a typical, tough Victorian explorer who had few fears of the dangers, such as crocodiles, that she faced.

### Crocodile attack
Mary Kingsley never made a drama out of danger. Once, when paddling her canoe in a swamp, a crocodile "chose to get his front paws over the stern of my canoe, and endeavoured to improve our acquaintance." So she "had to retire to the bows…and fetch him a clip on the snout with a paddle," and he then withdrew.

The Victorian age was one of the great periods of exploration and discovery. By 1837 – when Victoria became Queen of England – the coastlines of most parts of the world were no mystery. However, there were still large, empty spaces on maps.

To Europeans, the interior of central Africa was one such blank. The Europeans who came to explore it mostly did so because they were simply interested in finding out what was there. However, nearly all of them also became fascinated with the region itself – as well as with the excitement and surprise of exploration.

Many of these explorers, such as Mary Kingsley, went either alone or with just one other European companion, but most were accompanied by a party of local porters, interpreters, and guides. Although the European explorers in Africa were usually men, individual women who had money and a sense of adventure also went exploring.

There were few roads and dense jungle in many places, so rivers were a major route into "Darkest Africa," as the continent was called. The Niger,

**Above** This sketch shows David Livingstone's canoe being upset by a hippopotamus while he was exploring Africa.

Nile, Zambezi, and Congo (now called Zaire) rivers became star attractions for Victorian explorers.

The biggest puzzle was where these rivers started. This question was an irresistible challenge for the Victorians, and some were determined to solve it whatever the odds. Samuel Baker, an English explorer who with his wife Florence von Sass traveled for years in Africa, said, "nothing but death shall prevent me from discovering the sources of the Nile." In fact he, along with others, was beaten to it by John Hanning Speke in 1858.

Finding the source of the Nile became the main aim in life for another explorer, the Scotsman David Livingstone. He knew Africa and its hazards, but on an expedition begun in 1866 he lost contact with his traveling companions. Over five years he traveled from Lake Nyasa

**Faithful guides**
European explorers could not have made their journeys without the help of local people who acted as interpreters, guides, guards, porters, and cooks. John Hanning Speke employed an African named "Bombay," who he said was "the life and success of the expedition." Bombay accompanied Speke through all the hardships, and they reached Lake Victoria together. Later he accompanied Stanley on his search for Livingstone.

### Stanley crosses Africa

From 1874 to 1877 Henry Stanley made one of the greatest journeys in the history of African exploration, crossing from Zanzibar on the east coast of Africa to the mouth of the Congo River on the west coast in 999 days. His party suffered terrible hardships, many dying of disease or from attacks by tribespeople. Boats had to be carried around rapids and waterfalls, and they struggled through dense, hot rain forest.

on to Lake Tanganyika, exploring the lakes and rivers in the area. Eventually he became sick and exhausted and returned to Lake Tanganyika in 1871 seeking supplies. He was thought to be dead. It took another great explorer to find him – the journalist Henry Stanley, who was sent by *The New York Herald*. He greeted the missing explorer with the famous words, "Dr. Livingstone, I presume?"

Victorian explorers usually kept diaries of their travels. Many of the details were of specialist scientific interest, but several explorers wrote in a style that the ordinary person could enjoy. They published books that

**Below** The famous meeting when Henry Stanley (left) finally found David Livingstone, who had been missing in Africa for nearly five years.

became very fashionable, and newspapers started to follow their travels. Some explorers became heroes.

The discussion about where the source of the Nile lay was particularly popular. Two explorers – Richard Burton and John Hanning Speke – claimed to have found it. They had both traced rivers and lakes in East Africa that could be the source, and Speke assumed it was Lake Victoria. (He was correct.) Burton thought it was Lake Tanganyika. A public debate was organized to settle the matter, but Speke died in a hunting accident on the morning it was due to take place.

# To the ends of the Earth

## The Arctic

Few explorers had ventured far into the frozen wastes of the Arctic until the last part of the nineteenth century. Because both polar regions now seemed to be the last places on Earth left to explore, many countries wanted to be the first to find out more about the great ice masses and in particular to reach the poles themselves. The idea of a "race for the pole" excited the public, and newspapers kept people in touch with the latest events of the various expeditions.

The Arctic is all sea, permanently frozen over around the North Pole. At first, exploration of the area was kept to the surrounding islands, since it was impossible to get a boat anywhere near the floating and shifting polar ice cap. Many nations, especially those that lay within reach of the area, raised money for expeditions that were scientific as well as

**Above** The American, Robert Peary, was a U.S. Navy officer who had spent many years exploring the Arctic region before his successful attempt to reach the North Pole.

exploratory, but they were unable to reach the pole.

Robert Peary, an American, had a lifelong ambition to reach the North Pole. For over twenty years he prepared himself, exploring Greenland, becoming a sledding expert, and learning survival skills

from the Inuit people. He made several attempts to get to the pole; after one expedition, he had to have most of his toes removed because of frostbite.

His determination, as well as advances in technology, finally helped him reach his goal. From a special ship built to withstand the ice, *The Roosevelt*, he made his final assault in February 1909 with just one other American, Matthew Henson, and a small group of Inuit guides, plus the bare minimum of food and dogsleds. He reached the North Pole on April 6, 1909.

North Pole (April 6, 1909)

Route taken by
Robert Peary

Ellesmere Island

GREENLAND

Dressed in thick furs against the
bitter cold, Robert Peary led the first
team of explorers to reach the North
Pole. With him were his dogsled
driver, Matthew Henson, and a few
Inuit guides.

### The Antarctic

People had puzzled for hundreds of years over the question of whether there was a southern continent, but it was not until 1820 that the landmass of the Antarctic was finally sighted. Although scientific expeditions sailed to the edge, it was 1895 before anyone started to explore the interior.

In 1911, the race to be the first to reach the South Pole was on. At two different points on the Ross Ice Shelf, Roald Amundsen from Norway and Robert Scott from England waited for the dark and bitter Antarctic winter to pass. They had both made polar attempts before.

Amundsen decided to use dogs to haul his sleds, but Scott's team at first relied on Siberian ponies and then on their own efforts to pull their supplies. In October 1911 Amundsen set off through blinding snow with four companions and his team of fifty-two dogs. Even in

**Above** Lieutenant Helmer Hansen with his dog team standing at the South Pole marked by the Norwegian flag. This photograph was taken by Amundsen.

summer the temperatures were minus 22°F.

A long 9,750-foot climb took them up onto the Polar Plateau. In terrible weather they crossed the Devil's Ballroom, where hollow floors of ice could

**Dog power**
As Amundsen said later, "The greatest difference between Scott's and my equipment lay undoubtedly in our choice of draught animals." Using dogs rather than ponies (and later men) to pull the sleds was vital in the very tough climb up onto the Polar Plateau.

The dogs were also a source of fresh meat – Amundsen's expedition killed twenty-four of them for food.

suddenly give way. After two months they reached the South Pole and then made a safe return to base.

Scott and five companions arrived at the pole about a month later to find Amundsen's Norwegian flag. Extremely disappointed, he struggled back toward base with his

**Sleds**
Even with modern equipment available, sleds have always been used by polar explorers to carry supplies and equipment. The early ones, based on the Inuit *komatik*, were light and flexible and could be pulled by dogs.

men suffering from frostbite and lack of food. Finally, caught in a blizzard just 11 miles from base Scott wrote, "These rough notes and our dead bodies must tell the tale." The bodies were found in November 1912.

**Right** Scott and his weary team arrive at the South Pole to find that Amundsen had reached it before them. They stopped to take this photograph (Scott is standing in the middle) before the attempt to get back to base.

One of the great polar leaders and explorers of the time was Ernest Shackleton who, although he led many expeditions in the Antarctic, never reached the South Pole itself. He used modern inventions to help in exploration, such as a car designed to haul sleds over the ice. He was also the first person to use a motion-picture camera in the Antarctic.

New developments in technology brought new ways to explore. In the Arctic, Amundsen was one of those to pioneer flights both in airships and in airplanes.

The airplane had a great impact on exploration of the poles. Barriers of ice and snow could be crossed quickly and relatively comfortably. The first airplanes were used in the Antarctic in 1928, to map huge areas of previously unknown land. They were also used on expeditions to shift men and supplies.

**Great ocean wave**
In 1914 Ernest Shackleton planned to cross the Antarctic continent, but, before he even began, his ship was crushed in the ice of the Antarctic seas. In a tiny open whaling boat he and five others successfully crossed eight hundred miles of wild sea in search of help for his ship's crew who were stranded on an island. At one moment he looked up and saw a gigantic wave coming down on them: "It was a mighty upheaval of the ocean, a thing apart from the big white-capped seas that had been our tireless enemies for many days…We felt our boat lifted and flung forward like a cork in breaking surf." Eventually, Shackleton reached land and led the expedition that rescued his crew.

**Left** Ernest Shackleton, from England, was one of the most experienced explorers in the Antarctic. In 1908 he nearly reached the South Pole but, only 93 miles from his goal, he had to turn back because of bad weather.

# The final frontier

With the famous words "That's one small step for [a] man, one giant leap for mankind," on July 20, 1969 Neil Armstrong stepped on to the surface of the moon. Beyond the horizon he could see the small blue globe of Earth, 235,600 miles away.

Every moment of the flight to the moon in the *Apollo 11* spacecraft was carefully monitored and controlled by computers. The risks were as high as any explorer had faced before, but the advanced technology of the twentieth century meant that each danger could be calculated beforehand and precautions could be taken.

Even so, the first lunar mission was not without alarms. As the module came down to land on the moon, the computer on board failed, and Armstrong had to take manual control. People at mission control held their breath as he desperately searched for a place to set down that was not covered

**Above** On July 20, 1969 the manned spacecraft *Apollo 11* lifted off into space, opening a new era of exploration and discovery.

with boulders. The craft landed with only a few seconds of fuel left.

Neil Armstrong and Edwin "Buzz" Aldrin were watched by millions of people as they walked on the moon. For the first time, one of the great moments in the history of exploration could be seen live on television by people sitting at home.

## Floating around

Armstrong had been an astronaut since 1962 and so was quite relaxed on the flight to the moon. Speaking from the spacecraft, he said, "I have been having a ball floating around inside here back and forth from one place to another...sure is nice in here. I've been very busy so far. I'm looking towards taking the afternoon off, I've been cooking and sweeping ...well, you know the usual housekeeping things."

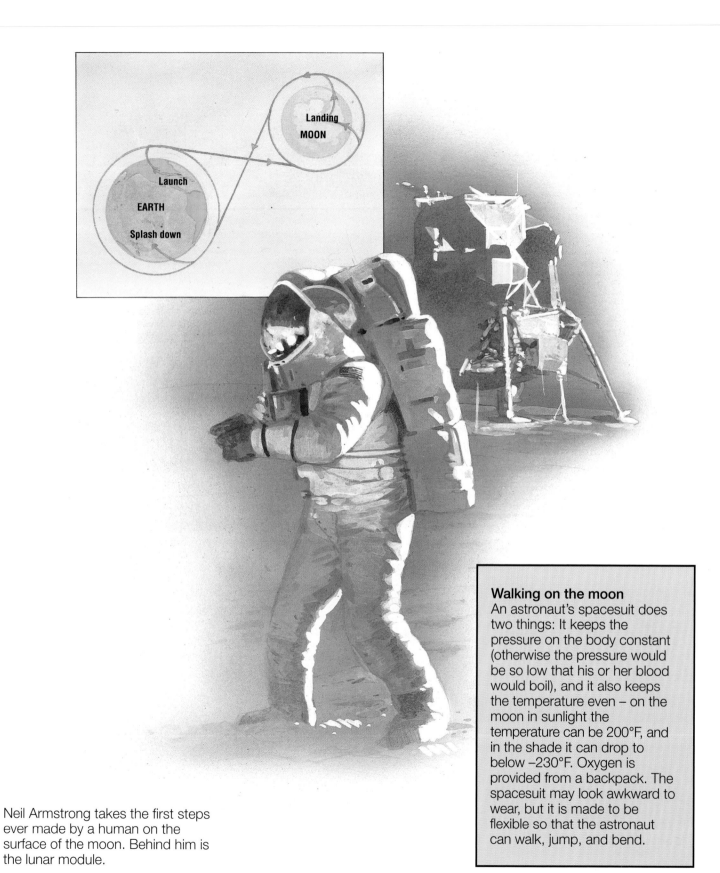

Landing
MOON

Launch

EARTH

Splash down

**Walking on the moon**
An astronaut's spacesuit does two things: It keeps the pressure on the body constant (otherwise the pressure would be so low that his or her blood would boil), and it also keeps the temperature even – on the moon in sunlight the temperature can be 200°F, and in the shade it can drop to below –230°F. Oxygen is provided from a backpack. The spacesuit may look awkward to wear, but it is made to be flexible so that the astronaut can walk, jump, and bend.

Neil Armstrong takes the first steps ever made by a human on the surface of the moon. Behind him is the lunar module.

# The final frontier

Although for centuries people had dreamed about leaving Earth, it was only the scientific knowledge of the twentieth century that made it possible. Missiles that had been developed for war could, if powerful enough, become rockets to reach space.

After World War II (1939 – 1945), scientists from the United States and the then-Soviet Union used this missile technology independently to create the first spacecraft. The Soviets surprised everyone by being the first to launch a

**Above** Yuri Gagarin became the first person to travel in space on April 12, 1961 in the spaceship *Vostok I*.

satellite in October 1957. This was *Sputnik I*. Four years later, they were the first to launch a person into space – Yuri Gagarin.

The "space race" was on. The Americans launched a man into space a year later in 1962; the Soviets sent the first woman, Valentina Tereshkova, up in 1963; in 1965 a Soviet made the first space walk. The Americans managed the first moon landing in 1969, and the first reusable space shuttle was launched in 1981. Since then there have been many manned and unmanned flights, not only by Americans and Soviets, but by astronauts and spacecraft from other countries, too.

### Space shuttle
Building spacecraft is very expensive. The Americans designed the reusable space shuttle to help cut costs. Fired by rocket boosters that can be recovered, the shuttle reaches Earth's orbit. Small engines allow it to maneuver in space. It can orbit for up to thirty days, has a cargo bay, and can carry satellites. On reentering Earth's atmosphere, it glides down to the surface. The runway has to be about three miles long, because the shuttle has no brakes and lands at 340 miles per hour.

Space shuttles could be very useful for future exploration of our planet and space. They can launch space probes, and they could help with the construction of space stations.

One of the initial reasons for the interest in space exploration was scientific and general curiosity. But it was also spurred by the race between the U.S. and the Soviet Union to beat each other into space. The two nations had military reasons for spending vast amounts of money on the space program: they hoped to send up spy satellites and even weapons to orbit Earth.

Placing satellites in space is one of the main reasons today that rockets are launched. These satellites help with weather forecasting or can be used as link-ups for communication around the world. Some carry out studies and surveys of Earth. As well as satellite launches, flights are made to carry out scientific experiments in the special environmental conditions of space.

Exploration has become so technologically advanced now that we are able to send robots to do our searching for us. They are cheaper to build than manned craft and can reach far into space. They can send information back to Earth by radio waves. Unmanned space probes

**Above** An artist's impression of the *Voyager* probe passing the rings of Saturn while on its mission to explore our solar system.

such as *Voyager* explored our solar system (the nine planets that orbit the sun). The *Pioneer* space probes have been the first to go beyond our system and travel through other solar systems and galaxies. They carry simple messages about Earth in case other civilizations discover them.

Further advances in technology are needed before humans can be sent on these voyages. The journeys are long – it could take more than a year to reach Mars – but a year's journey is nothing compared to the great voyages of some of the explorers of the past. For an explorer, space is the ultimate dream because it has no limit, so there will always be something new to find.

**The Beauty of Earth**
Nearly all the two hundred or so astronauts who have seen Earth from space have marveled at the sight. The Russian Alexei Leonov said, "The Earth looked so blue and so round, and so small, so delicate." After returning from a Soviet mission, Sigmund Jahn, from the former East Germany, declared "Before I flew I was already aware of how small and vulnerable our planet is. But only when I saw it from space, in all its ...beauty and fragility, did I realize that humankind's most urgent task is to cherish and preserve it for future generations."

# Glossary

**Altitude**   The height of an object above a certain level, usually sea level.

**Antarctic**   The area surrounding the South Pole.

**Arctic**   The area surrounding the North Pole.

**Astrolabe**   An instrument used by sailors to work out the position of the sun and stars – and therefore work out their own location.

**Astronauts**   People who travel in space.

**Byzantine**   The Roman Empire in the East. Its capital was Constantinople (now called Istanbul). The Byzantine Empire existed until 1453, long after the decline of the Roman Empire in the west.

**Caravan**   A group of people traveling together, often for safety.

**Chronometer**   An accurate timepiece that was used to keep time at sea.

**Colonists**   People who form a settlement in a country far from their homeland.

**Conquistadores**   The Spanish soldiers who explored South and Central America.

**Dark Ages**   A period from the fifth to the tenth century in Europe when there were few new ideas or thoughts.

**Dynasty**   A long line of rulers, often from the same family.

**Era**   An historical period.

**Far East**   A general name for countries in eastern Asia, including China and Japan (but not India).

**Frostbite**   Damage to the body (sometimes causing death) from becoming too cold in freezing temperatures.

**Hemisphere**   The two halves of the planet, north and south of the equator.

**Latitude**   Position to the north or south of the equator (the imaginary line around the middle of the earth).

**Leeches**   Bloodsucking, wormlike creatures that live in warm and wet places.

**Middle Ages**   The period of time in Europe after the fall of the Roman Empire and before the Renaissance (from the fifth to about the fifteenth century).

**Middle East**   A general name for countries of the eastern Mediterranean, particularly the Arab countries.

**Missionaries**   Members of religious groups who go to foreign countries to do religious work.

**Monitored**   Checked regularly.

**Muslim**   A person who follows the Islamic religion, which was founded by the prophet Muhammad in the seventh century A.D.

**Navigation**   Planning the route of a ship or any other vehicle and keeping it on course.

**New World**   An old European term for North and South America.

**North Star**   A fixed star by which sailors can find their direction at night.

**Pagan**   A person who does not follow the Christian, Jewish, or Islamic religion.

**Plunder**   To steal.

**Pope**   The head of the Roman Catholic Church.

**Porcelain**   A very fine kind of pottery or china, first made in China.

**Pyre**   A heap or pile of materials that burn.

**Satellite**   A machine that humans have put into space to help send communications around the world or to carry out scientific experiments.

**Scurvy**   A disease that can kill, caused by the lack of vitamin C. Sailors on long voyages did not eat enough fresh fruit and vegetables, which contain vitamin C.

**Sextant**   A navigational instrument that helped sailors to figure out in what direction they were sailing.

**Soviet Union**   The former group of republics in Eastern Europe and Northern Asia that were governed by the Supreme Soviet (overall council) based in Moscow. The Soviet Union broke into separate states in 1991.

**Victorian**   A person who lived in England during the reign of Queen Victoria (1837–1901).

# Further reading

*The Age of Exploration*. North Bellmore, NY: Marshall Cavendish, 1990.

Baker, Susan. *Explorers of North America*. Tales of Courage. Austin: Raintree Steck-Vaughn, 1990.

Chrisp, Peter. *Search for the East*. Explorations and Encounters. New York: Thomson Learning, 1993.

Chrisp, Peter. *Voyages to the New World*. Explorations and Encounters. New York: Thomson Learning, 1993.

Gaines, Ann. *Herodotus and the Explorers of the Classical Age*. New York: Chelsea House, 1993.

Grant, Neil. *The Great Atlas of Discovery*. New York: Alfred A. Knopf Books for Young Readers, 1992.

Grosseck, Joyce and Atwood, Elizabeth. *Great Explorers*. Rev. ed. Grand Rapids: Gateway Press, 1988.

Haskins, Jim. *Against All Opposition: Black Explorers in America*. New York: Walker & Co., 1992.

Lomask, Milton. *Great Lives: Exploration*. Macmillan Children's Book Group, 1988.

Martini, Teri. *Christopher Columbus: The Man Who Unlocked the Secrets of the World*. Mahwah, NJ: Paulist Press, 1992.

Matthews, Rupert. *Explorer*. New York: Alfred A. Knopf Books for Young Readers, 1991.

# Timeline

Some important dates in the history of exploration

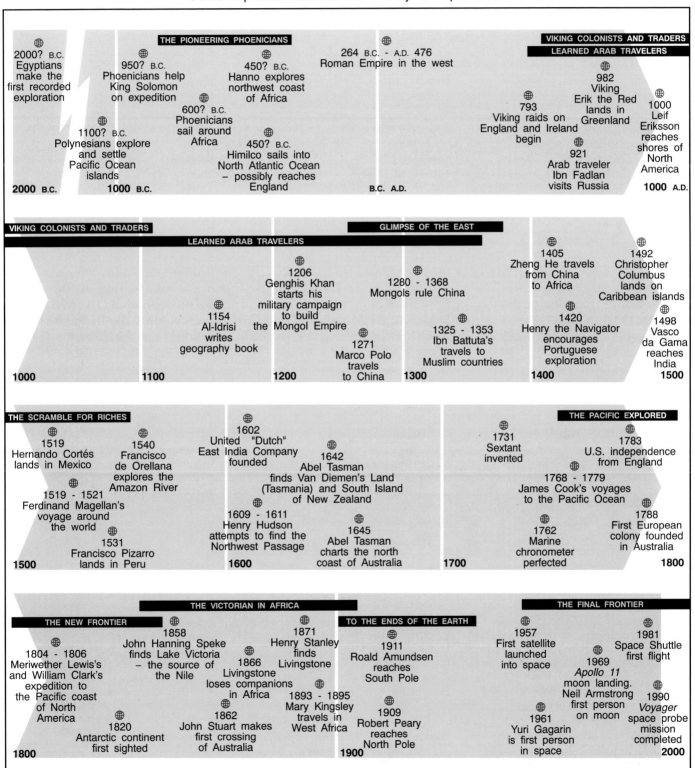

**THE PIONEERING PHOENICIANS**

**VIKING COLONISTS AND TRADERS**

**LEARNED ARAB TRAVELERS**

2000? B.C.
Egyptians make the first recorded exploration

950? B.C.
Phoenicians help King Solomon on expedition

450? B.C.
Hanno explores northwest coast of Africa

264 B.C. - A.D. 476
Roman Empire in the west

982
Viking Erik the Red lands in Greenland

793
Viking raids on England and Ireland begin

1000
Leif Eriksson reaches shores of North America

600? B.C.
Phoenicians sail around Africa

1100? B.C.
Polynesians explore and settle Pacific Ocean islands

450? B.C.
Himilco sails into North Atlantic Ocean – possibly reaches England

921
Arab traveler Ibn Fadlan visits Russia

2000 B.C.      1000 B.C.      B.C. A.D.      1000 A.D.

---

**VIKING COLONISTS AND TRADERS**

**LEARNED ARAB TRAVELERS**

**GLIMPSE OF THE EAST**

1206
Genghis Khan starts his military campaign to build the Mongol Empire

1280 - 1368
Mongols rule China

1405
Zheng He travels from China to Africa

1492
Christopher Columbus lands on Caribbean islands

1154
Al-Idrisi writes geography book

1271
Marco Polo travels to China

1325 - 1353
Ibn Battuta's travels to Muslim countries

1420
Henry the Navigator encourages Portuguese exploration

1498
Vasco da Gama reaches India

1000      1100      1200      1300      1400      1500

---

**THE SCRAMBLE FOR RICHES**

**THE PACIFIC EXPLORED**

1519
Hernando Cortés lands in Mexico

1540
Francisco de Orellana explores the Amazon River

1602
United "Dutch" East India Company founded

1642
Abel Tasman finds Van Diemen's Land (Tasmania) and South Island of New Zealand

1731
Sextant invented

1783
U.S. independence from England

1519 - 1521
Ferdinand Magellan's voyage around the world

1531
Francisco Pizarro lands in Peru

1609 - 1611
Henry Hudson attempts to find the Northwest Passage

1645
Abel Tasman charts the north coast of Australia

1768 - 1779
James Cook's voyages to the Pacific Ocean

1762
Marine chronometer perfected

1788
First European colony founded in Australia

1500      1600      1700      1800

---

**THE VICTORIAN IN AFRICA**

**THE FINAL FRONTIER**

**THE NEW FRONTIER**

**TO THE ENDS OF THE EARTH**

1858
John Hanning Speke finds Lake Victoria – the source of the Nile

1871
Henry Stanley finds Livingstone

1911
Roald Amundsen reaches South Pole

1957
First satellite launched into space

1981
Space Shuttle first flight

1804 - 1806
Meriwether Lewis's and William Clark's expedition to the Pacific coast of North America

1866
Livingstone loses companions in Africa

1969
Apollo 11 moon landing. Neil Armstrong first person on moon

1990
Voyager space probe mission completed

1893 - 1895
Mary Kingsley travels in West Africa

1909
Robert Peary reaches North Pole

1820
Antarctic continent first sighted

1862
John Stuart makes first crossing of Australia

1961
Yuri Gagarin is first person in space

1800      1900      2000

# Index

## Sources of quotations

**p. 6** Phoenician ship, **p. 7** Land of Flames, and **p. 8** Around Africa quotes are all from *A History of Discovery and Exploration: The Search Begins* (Aldus Books/Jupiter Books, 1973) pages 166, 61, and 41 respectively. **p. 12** Raid and Viking traders quotes are from pages 65 and 100 in *The Voyage of Discovery* by Crone and Kendall (Wayland Publishers, 1970). **p. 14** Caravan, **p. 16** Wealthy traveler, and **p. 17** Travel stories quotes are all from *Ibn Battuta: Travels in Asia and Africa* (Routledge and Kegan Paul, 1983) pages 73, 197, and 101 respectively. **p. 21** Strange creatures quote is from page 149 of *Marco Polo: The Travels* translated by R. Latham (Penguin Books, 1975). **p. 22** Inca

civilization, **p. 23** Inca defeat and **p. 24** Destruction of a race quotes are all from *Explorers* by Desmond Wilcox (BBC Books, 1975) pages 200, 186-7, and 219 respectively. **p. 25** The quote on the Amazon basin is from page 140 of *A History of Discovery and Exploration: The New World* (Aldus Books/Jupiter Books, 1973). **p. 26** Healthy cabbage, **p. 28** A skilled mapmaker, and **p. 29** Friendly islanders quotes are all from *The Travels of Captain Cook* by Ronald Symes (Michael Joseph, 1972) pages 40, 61, and 101 respectively. **p. 30** Wet Pacific quote comes from page 208 of *The Discoverers: An Encyclopedia of Explorers and Exploration* by Helen Delpar (McGraw-Hill, 1980). **p. 34**

Mary Kingsley and Cannibals quotes are from pages 119/102 and 117 of *Explorers* by Desmond Wilcox (BBC Books, 1975). **p. 35** Crocodile attack quote is from page 63 of *The Life of Mary Kingsley* by Stephen Gwynn (Macmillan, 1932). **p. 40** Dog power quote comes from page 13 of *Explorers* by Desmond Wilcox (BBC Books, 1975). **p. 41** Great ocean wave quote is from page 13 of *The World Atlas of Exploration* by Eric Newby (Mitchell Beazley, 1975). **p. 42** Floating around and **p. 43** Walking on the Moon quotes are from *Apollo 11 Moon Landing* by David J. Shayler (Ian Allen, 1989). **p. 45** The beauty of Earth comes from page 32 of *For All Mankind* by Harry Hurt III (Macdonald, 1989).